# QUEEN
## OF THE
# FALLS

## Chris Van Allsburg

Houghton Mifflin Books for Children
Houghton Mifflin Harcourt
Boston  New York  2010

I magine being as small as a flea, standing on a sidewalk next to an open fire hydrant. This is how visitors to the waterfalls at Niagara feel. The water drops from a height that is as tall as a seventeen-story building, roaring like a locomotive and sending up an endless cloud of mist as it crashes onto the rocks and water below. The earth at its base practically shakes, terrifying and thrilling anyone who goes there.

A visitor to Niagara back in the year 1901 would have found towns built on both sides of the falls, with many hotels that held the trainloads of people that arrived each day. Tourists usually filled the sidewalks, restaurants, and horse-drawn carriages. However, midday on October 24 of that year, the streets and sidewalks were strangely deserted. On that cool autumn Monday, all of Niagara had gathered at the edge of the falls. There in the mist, a restless crowd of thousands waited impatiently.

Suddenly voices shouted, "There it is!" Outstretched hands pointed to the crest of the cascading wall of water. For a fleeting moment a large barrel was visible, and then it plunged over the falls, disappearing in a liquid avalanche. Many in the crowd cried out; then all eyes were frozen on the churning water below.

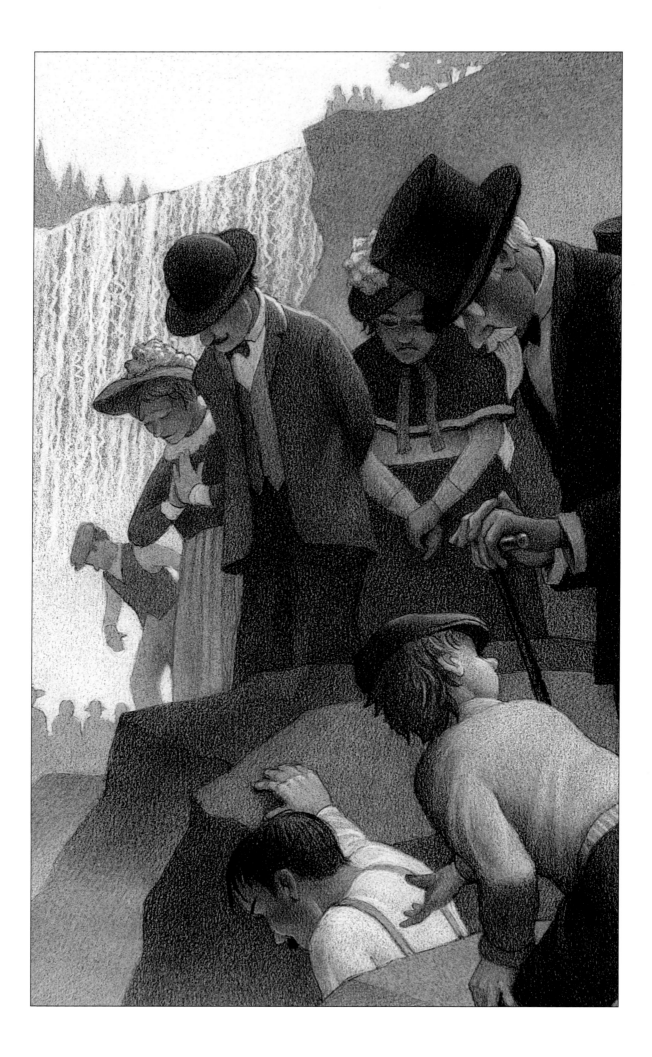

Why had so many people gathered to watch a barrel plunge over the waterfall? Wouldn't the tons of water pounding onto the rocks below have simply broken it to pieces? And yet there they stood, watching and waiting, holding their breath—waiting, because they all knew the barrel was not empty.

**Bay City, Michigan,** was a logging town located two hundred miles west of Niagara Falls. On its Main Street, tucked in between the shops and offices, was a charm school, a place where the children of Bay City's finest families could learn the correct fork to use at dinner, the usefulness of handkerchiefs, and how to properly dance the waltz.

The school's owner and only teacher was a short, plump, and fussy sixty-two-year-old widow named Annie Edson Taylor.

For many years, she had traveled around America, from Chattanooga to Charleston to San Antonio, offering classes in dance and fine manners.

Finally, her travels led her to Bay City, where more than one hundred children enrolled in her new school. But her success did not last. As Annie grew older and her classes grew smaller, she was forced to say goodbye to her final student and close the school.

Sitting in the place she called home, a small room in a boarding house, Annie worried about her future. She had not saved very much money during her years of traveling and teaching. Now she was frightened she might end up in the poorhouse, an unhappy place where old people without money or a family to care for them went to live out their years.

She thought about looking for ordinary work as a store clerk or a cleaning woman, but Annie could not picture herself standing behind a counter selling candy to her former students, or scrubbing the floors in their parents' homes. She was too proud, and the pay she would earn, too little. What Annie needed was a plan, a way to strike it rich and put her money worries behind her for good.

Days passed by and the widow's small savings grew even smaller. Try as she might, Annie could not come up with an idea, until one warm July evening when she returned to her room with a newspaper. The front page carried a story about the large number of tourists visiting Niagara Falls that summer. Annie had visited the falls as a child and could remember, clearly, the thundering waters and crowds of people drawn to them. Holding her father's hand, she had been hypnotized by the sight and sound.

Suddenly, like a cork popping from a champagne bottle, an idea came to her. She would find fame and fortune by doing something no one in the world had ever done before. Annie Taylor would go over Niagara Falls in a barrel.

The next morning, filled with excitement, Annie began planning her ride. She knew no ordinary barrel would do. Something special was called for. Annie drew a picture of a barrel that would suit her needs, a barrel that would be incredibly strong and just the right size for its passenger.

She took her drawing to a workshop where men built barrels, mostly for holding things such as pickles and beer. The foreman of the shop had never seen a barrel like the one Annie had drawn and asked what it was for.

When she shared her plans to ride in the barrel over Niagara Falls, the man looked at Annie in disbelief. He handed the drawing back and informed her his shop would build no such thing. The idea was madness, he told her. If she wanted to kill herself, she'd have to do it on her own.

Annie went back to her room and continued to dream of the fame and fortune that would be hers once she'd conquered the falls. She looked at her drawing and was certain she would be safe no matter how violent the ride.

Three days later, Annie called on the barrel maker again and convinced him she was not crazy. If he built the barrel according to her design, the widow assured him, she could survive the fall without injury. The foreman agreed to do it and put his three best men on the job.

Annie worked alongside them, picking out each piece of the thick white oak they used. When their work was done, they had a barrel that was four and a half feet high, with iron bands wrapped around it, and weighed more than one hundred and sixty pounds.

The workmen agreed, it was a very sturdy thing indeed. It might even go through the falls in one piece. That didn't mean, of course, that anyone inside would survive.

Annie understood the problem: You can put an egg inside a can and let it drop to the floor. The can may not be damaged, but it's a different story for the egg. That was why Annie made the barrel just big enough to hold herself and a large number of pillows. She also fastened to the inside metal handles to grab on to, and a leather belt to strap herself in securely.

As Annie put the finishing touches on the barrel, she began planning her trip. She needed a manager, someone to go to Niagara Falls ahead of her and stir up interest among the local newspaper reporters and tell them about the amazing lady daredevil who would be arriving soon to conquer the mighty falls.

She hired Frank Russell, a Bay City man who had worked at carnivals and fairs. When they first met, Frank Russell was surprised by Annie's appearance. She looked exactly like the aging charm school teacher that she was and nothing at all like the death-defying daredevil she was determined to become.

He asked if she wasn't too old for such a difficult and dangerous adventure. Even a much stronger and fitter person stood practically no chance of surviving what she proposed. Annie had already decided that the public would have greater interest in a daredevil more youthful then herself, so she told him that she was only forty-two, instantly erasing twenty years from her true age.

Mr. Russell didn't really believe her, and he didn't think anyone else would either. He did believe, though, that she was determined to go over the falls, and was certain there was money to be made if by some miracle she managed to climb out of her barrel alive.

He could then parade Annie across America, visiting lecture halls and theaters, where people would pay to see the barrel and to hear her tell her story. Both he and Annie could get rich. Frank Russell accepted her offer and set off for Niagara Falls to set the stage for her arrival.

Getting newspapers to run stories about Annie was not the only thing her manager needed to do. He also had to hire someone who could put Annie and her barrel in the river above the falls. If Annie was to have any chance of surviving her trip, the barrel would have to be placed in the water at exactly the right spot.

Fred Truesdale lived in a cottage on the river's bank not far from the falls and knew the river as well as any man. He had a sturdy boat and the muscles to row it through the river's swift and deadly currents. He agreed to set the barrel and its passenger into the river.

When Annie and her barrel finally arrived in Niagara, Frank

Russell made sure there were newspaper reporters at the train station. Because he had stretched the truth a good deal by describing Annie as a forty-two-year-old adventuress who climbed mountains and swam across frigid lakes, the reporters were expecting a different sort of woman from the one who stepped off the train.

Many of them wondered if the promised trip over the falls was just some kind of hoax: The barrel might go over, but would it really carry Annie Taylor inside? She looked old enough to be someone's grandmother and appeared to have spent considerably more time baking pies than climbing mountains.

As Annie answered their questions, directly and sincerely, the reporters began to think she might be telling the truth. Maybe this woman, as incredible and ridiculous as it seemed, would actually climb into her barrel and go where no man or woman had gone before.

The reporters went back to their newspapers, the barrel was put on display in Niagara's largest hotel, and Annie went with Frank to the boarding house where he'd taken rooms for them.

Frank Russell decided that Annie should wait ten days before taking her plunge over the falls. This would allow for excitement and interest to build up in the public, as they read the newspaper stories about "the fearless Mrs. Taylor" and viewed her barrel in the hotel lobby.

When the fateful day arrived, Annie and Frank took a carriage to the riverside cottage of Fred Truesdale, the boatman. Annie's barrel, delivered from the hotel, waited for her there, along with a number of reporters and a small crowd of curious onlookers. Much larger crowds had gathered downriver around the falls, not sure if they would see a miracle that day or a tragedy.

Fred Truesdale and his assistant, Billy Holleran, put the barrel in Fred's boat. They helped Annie aboard, and as they rowed out into the river, the reporters and spectators cheered and called out, "Good luck, Mrs. Taylor!" She stood in the boat and waved. "I will not say goodbye," she told them, "for I know I will see you all shortly." Then Annie sat back down and adjusted her long black skirt, smiling politely at Fred and Billy.

As the two men pulled their oars, she could hear the falls' loud and angry roar, even from a mile away.

There was a small island downriver, closer to the falls. Fred Truesdale guided his boat to it, and once ashore he and Billy lifted the barrel off the boat and laid it sideways on dry ground.

Annie, ever proud and proper, asked the men to turn away as she removed her hat and jacket, then got down on her hands and knees and backed into the open barrel. She strapped herself in, then had the boatman hand her the pillows she'd brought along. Once Annie was tightly packed inside, she told Fred Truesdale to seal up the barrel. As he and Billy put the lid in place, Annie said, "So long, boys." Then they pounded the cover down, fastened it with screws, and rolled the barrel into the water. Billy tied one end of a rope to the barrel and the other end to the boat.

The men rowed away from the island, drawing close to the "Point of No Return," a place where the river ran so quickly on its way to the falls that no boat could escape its pull.

Fred Truesdale tapped on the barrel with his oar and told Annie he was going to cut the rope. Her muffled voice answered back, "All righty." The line was cut and the two boatmen rowed with all their strength, fighting the fierce current that quickly stole the barrel away.

Along the shoreline, waiting crowds spotted Annie's barrel, carried along in a raging river that became more violent as it raced toward the awful drop. The barrel spun and tumbled, slamming against rocks and waves, sometimes disappearing entirely from sight, sucked beneath the surface.

A shout went up—"Here she comes!"—that was repeated over and over, carrying the news downriver to the thousands waiting near the falls. The widow was on her way.

If Annie could have seen all the people who had come to watch her, she would have felt proud. It was exactly what she had hoped for. Inside the cold, wet barrel, though, Annie could feel only one thing: complete discombobulation. As she shot through the rapids that lead to the falls, she was upside down one second, on her side the next, then on her back. It was as if some angry giant were kicking the barrel toward the falls.

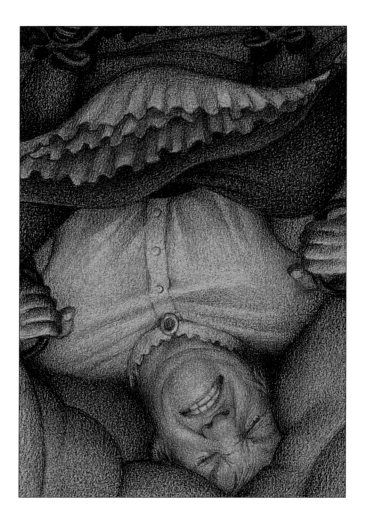

*Bang! Bang! Bang!* Yet Annie knew the worst was still to come.

Fred Truesdale had told her the water at the very edge of the falls would be still for a moment. When she felt that, he warned, she must hold on for dear life and pray.

Which was exactly what happened next. For a few seconds—one . . . two . . . three—Annie floated slowly and upright. She could hear the falls roaring, even through her thick oak barrel.

"Oh, Lord," she whispered, and then she was gone.

Some faint-hearted spectators screamed when they saw the barrel go over, others cheered, but most just stood silently with their mouths wide open and stared at the foaming water around the bottom of the falls. There was no sign of Annie, not even a piece of oak.

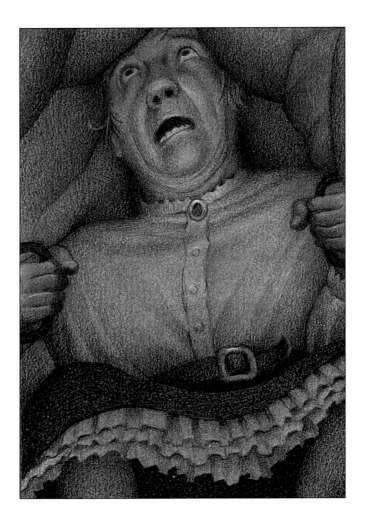

Suddenly the barrel bobbed to the surface. The crowd, still unsure of what had happened to its brave passenger, did not make a sound. When the barrel floated close to the rocky shore, men jumped into the water and lifted it onto the rocks. They knocked the lid off with a hammer.

One of the rescuers knelt down and stuck his head into the dark barrel, "Mrs. Taylor?" he asked. It was deadly silent. "Mrs. Taylor?" Then a weak voice spoke, "Where am I?" "Ma'am," the man answered, "you are over the falls."

Even with her rescuers' help, it took a while for Annie to squeeze out of the barrel. When she did, the crowd cheered. Annie waved back, but could barely lift her arm.

She was bruised and sore, had a cut on her forehead, and felt terribly dizzy. She was able to walk to a dock nearby, where Frank Russell had a carriage waiting.

Annie returned to her room at the boarding house. Doctors came to examine her and said she would have to stay in bed to recover from her injuries, which were not serious. Over the following days, newspaper reporters from around the country visited Annie. Soon her story was appearing in papers from New York to San Francisco. Americans could not have been more amazed if they'd read a horse had hit a home run, or a baby had been elected president. How could anyone, let alone a woman, survive a trip over Niagara Falls?

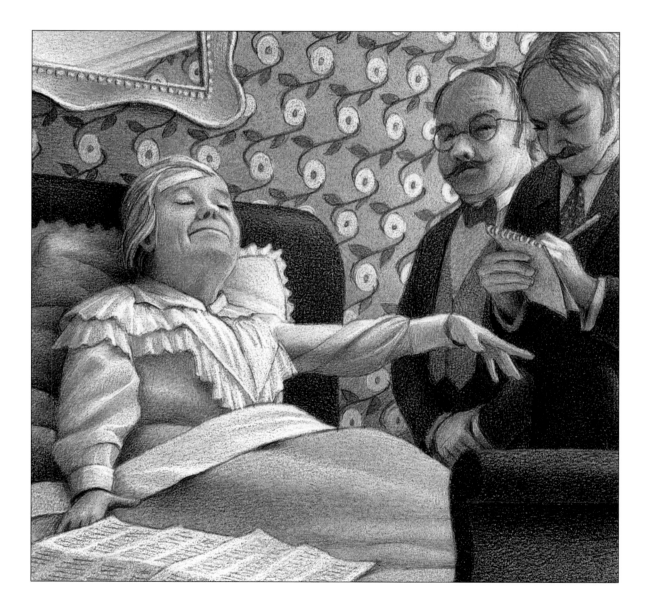

As soon as Annie felt well enough to travel, Frank Russell began to look for ways to make money. He took the widow to a large fair in nearby Buffalo. Hundreds of people lined up to buy tickets so they could see the amazing "Queen of the Falls."

When Annie took the stage beside her barrel, the audience was confused. Could this person in front of them, this grandma, really be the brave and fearless Mrs. Taylor who dared to ride over the waterfall? Annie told her story, but when she was done, there were no eager questions or loud applause. Everyone seemed to find the oak barrel more interesting than the woman who had ridden inside it.

When Annie was still back in Bay City, imagining her path to fame and fortune, she believed going over Niagara Falls in a barrel would be the hard part, but she was wrong.

Through the fall and winter of 1901, she and Frank Russell rode the train from one town to another, visiting lecture halls and theaters. The reaction to Annie was always the same. Excited crowds quickly lost interest when they discovered the fearless "Queen of the Falls" was a little old lady.

There were more and more empty seats in the theaters they visited. When it became clear to Frank Russell that he would not be getting rich with Annie, he ran off and, because he knew he could sell it, took her famous barrel with him. Fortunately Annie was able to get the barrel back, and to find herself a new manager named Billy Banks.

When summer arrived, Mr. Banks took Annie around to county fairs, where she took the stage in between the juggling acts and the hypnotist. The Queen of the Falls was not well received, and Billy Banks, just like Frank Russell, ended up stealing the barrel. He and a pretty young woman named Maggie Kaplan went ahead to the next fair on Annie's schedule, where Miss Kaplan pretended to be the Queen of the Falls. Annie put a stop to that but wasn't able to get her barrel back. Billy and Maggie ran off with it, and the thing was never seen again.

Annie went back to Niagara Falls, where she had another barrel built. She was determined to go out on the road again come spring, still searching for the pot of gold she believed was waiting for her. But when it came time to leave, she changed her mind. The widow had run out of steam.

She decided to place her new barrel in the park she'd visited as a child, near the falls. On a table in front of it, she displayed postcards of herself posing with the barrel and copies of a pamphlet she'd written about her life and famous ride. Calling out to tourists as they passed by, Annie invited them to purchase a postcard and to meet the Queen of the Falls.

When they approached and asked where the queen was, Annie had to work hard to convince them that they were looking at her.

Annie didn't think she would have to peddle postcards for long. She was certain someone who could help turn her fame into fortune would come along soon, but no one did. One summer selling souvenirs turned into many. Annie became a familiar figure to tourists passing through the park. Sitting in the shade of her barrel, she was always ready to tell her story.

One afternoon, a week before the tenth anniversary of her trip over the falls, she had a visitor at her souvenir stand. It was a newspaper reporter working on a story about her remarkable ride. The Queen of the Falls was happy to answer the questions he had for her, and the two of them sat on a bench overlooking the waterfall.

Annie admitted that following her ride things had not turned out as she had expected. "No, sir," she told the reporter, "I did not get rich from it, and that has been a disappointment. I won't deny it."

She stood up, took a few steps forward, and gazed at the falling water. "When I was nine years old," she said, "I stood here with my father, in this very spot. I'd never seen anything like that waterfall. It looked like the end of the world, beautiful and dreadful, all at once. My father took my hand and asked if I was frightened. I told him I was, then asked if we could get closer."

She turned back to the reporter. "That's what everyone wonders when they see Niagara," she went on. "How close will their courage let them get to it? Well, sir, you can't get any closer than I got. You ask any person who's stood here, looking out at those falls, what they thought of someone going over them in a barrel. Why, every last one would agree, it was the greatest feat ever performed."

"And I am content when I can say, 'I am the one who did it.'"

# Author's Note

October 1901; Niagara Falls (Ontario) Public Library

ANNIE EDSON TAYLOR was born in 1838 and died in 1921, twenty years after her extraordinary trip over the falls.

I first learned about this unusual woman in 1972 while reading a magazine article recounting the exploits of Niagara's daredevils. I was surprised I'd never heard of her and the remarkable trip that she had made. Over the years I've wondered why her story is not more widely known. When I decided to write about Annie, I believed I was undertaking a project quite different from the fantasies and surreal tales I'd become accustomed to creating. This was not the case. There is something decidedly fantastic and not quite real about Niagara Falls, about Annie's adventure, and about the stories that can unfold when imagination, determination, and foolhardiness combine to set humans off in pursuit of their goals.

Annie lived to see one other person accomplish what she had done when in 1911, Bobby Leach became the first man to survive the plunge. Since then, eight other individuals have successfully made the trip in vessels of various designs. A smaller number have done so unsuccessfully. Annie Taylor remains the only woman to have gone over the falls alone.

## Successful "Barrel" Riders

Annie Edson Taylor, 1901

Bobby Leach, 1911

Jean Lussier, 1928

William Fitzgerald (a.k.a. Nathan Boya), 1961

Karel Soucek, 1984

Steven Trotter, 1985

John "Super Dave" Munday, 1985, 1993

Peter De Bernardi and Jeffrey Petkovich (together), 1989

Steven Trotter and Lori Martin (together), 1995

## Bibliography

Berton, Pierre. *Niagara: A History of the Falls.* New York: Kodansha America, 1997.

Grant, John, and Ray Jones. *Niagara Falls: An Intimate Portrait.* Guilford: Globe Pequot Press, 2006.

Whalen, Dwight. *The Lady Who Conquered Niagara: The Annie Edson Taylor Story.* Brewer: EGA Books, 1990.

Houghton Mifflin Books for Children is an imprint of Houghton Mifflin Harcourt Publishing Company.

www.hmhbooks.com

Library of Congress Cataloging-in-Publication Number: 2010006780
ISBN 978-0-547-31581-2
Printed in Singapore
TWP 10 9 8 7 6 5 4 3 2 1
4500267639